BOOK ANALYSIS

By Sarah Barnett-Benelli

Claudius the God

BY ROBERT GRAVES

ROBERT GRAVES

ENGLISH NOVELIST, POET, BIOGRAPHER, TRANSLATOR

- **Born in Wimbledon in 1895.**
- **Died in Deyá in 1985.**
- **Notable works:**
  - *Goodbye to All That* (1929), autobiography
  - *The White Goddess: A Historical Grammar of Poetic Myth* (1948), myth and poetic inspiration
  - *Suetonius: The Twelve Caesars* (1957), translation

Born into a privileged background, Robert Graves was educated at Charterhouse School and Oxford University. At the outbreak of World War One he enlisted as an officer in the army and began to write the realistic war poems that first made him famous. Between 1916 and 1975 he wrote more than 120 books, including 55 collections of poetry and 15 novels. In 1929, after completing his autobiography, *Goodbye to All That*, he went with his then-partner Laura Riding to live in Majorca. In 1934 he was awarded the James Tait Black Memorial Prize for both *I, Claudius* and *Claudius the God* and the following year he was awarded the Hawthornden Prize for *I, Claudius*. He was married twice, first to the artist Nancy Nicholson, with whom he had four children, then to Beryl Hodge with whom he had another four.

CLAUDIUS THE GOD

SEQUEL TO *I, CLAUDIUS*

- **Genre:** historical novel
- **Reference edition:** Graves, R. (1978) *Claudius the God*. London: Penguin.
- **1st edition:** 1954
- **Themes:** power, empire, conquest, religion, rivalry, nepotism, family relationships

Claudius the God is the second of two historical novels presented as the autobiography of the Roman Emperor Claudius, who reigned between CE 41 and 54. As in the first book, we read of complex family relationships and bitter power struggles. Claudius had only survived the family feuds that led to the murder or banishment of so many of his relatives because he was considered to be a fool and not worth bothering with. Claudius had suffered from childhood with a number of health problems and stammered and limped. His ill-health had prevented him from becoming a soldier; nonetheless, as emperor he masterminded the conquest of Britain. He was unfortunate in his choice of wives, Messalina and Agrippillina, both of whom were able to manipulate him. The Claudius novels were a huge success, both with reviewers and the general public, and in 1976 were made into a BBC drama series starring Derek Jacobi.

SUMMARY

The novel opens with the Emperor Claudius recounting the dramatic events that had occurred at the end of the book's prequel, *I, Claudius*. His predecessor, the Emperor Caligula, had been assassinated and in the ensuing chaos Claudius was hoisted on to the shoulders of the palace guards and acclaimed emperor in his place. A Republican like his father and grandfather, Claudius did not want to be emperor, but at the urging of his young, pregnant wife Messalina he accepted his position. His friend King Herod Agrippa, who was in Rome at the time, counselled him that the alternative was civil war. The Senate did not initially accept Claudius, and Herod Agrippa warned him to be on his guard against assassination. He advised him not to enter the Senate house immediately and then only with armed guards.

The reign of the mad Emperor Caligula (who was Claudius' nephew) had been marked by cruelty and excessive spending, and the treasury coffers were empty. Claudius set about raising money by melting down the gold statues and ornaments that Caligula, who thought he was a god, had made for his own temple and converting them into gold coin. He removed the unreasonable taxes and edicts with which Caligula had burdened the people, and scaled down the cruel and expensive entertainments of which many were becoming weary. With his wife Messalina, who had a good political mind, he made changes in the government, putting people he trusted in important governmental posts. These included freedmen (former slaves) such as Pallas, Narcissus, Callistus and Polybius. Claudius valued the advice given to him by Herod Agrippa and encouraged him to stay in Rome a bit longer, promising to restore to him the lands lost by his grandfather, Herod the Great.

Claudius embarked on a number of important projects. He built two new aqueducts to bring fresh water into Rome and began work on draining Lake Fucine, in order to provide more farmland. He also ordered major improvements to the Port of Ostia. Rome was dependent on corn from Egypt, but often in the winter months ships could not get into the harbour, resulting in the loss of ships and crew and the all-important grain. A shortage of corn had led to riots among the people.

Claudius kept his promise to Herod Agrippa and confirmed his kingship of Bashan, Galilee and Gilead, and added to it Judea, Samaria and Edom. Before he returned home, Herod Agrippa advised Claudius to trust nobody. The two friends kept in touch, including personal letters among the official documents.

CONQUEST OF BRITAIN

Herod Agrippa wrote to Claudius suggesting he attempt a conquest of Britain. Britain had been invaded (but not conquered) by the dictator Julius Caesar in 55 BCE and again in 54 BCE. Claudius studied Julius Caesar's commentaries on his campaigns and planned his own expedition carefully. Caesar had taken 10 000 men on his first campaign and 20 000 on the second. Claudius sent four battalions (40 000 men) to Britain under the command of Aulus Plautius. He landed at Richborough on the East coast. The Kings of East Kent and East Sussex came to meet him with tokens of peace and swore alliance and friendship to Rome. Claudius had given orders that if any tribes submitted voluntarily to Rome, they would be given the privileges of subject allies. Magnanimity was to be shown to those captured. No property was to be destroyed unnecessarily, "nor women ravished, nor children or old people killed" (p. 230).

Aulus' goal was Colchester. They met with opposition from the armies of King Caractacus and his brother Togodumnus, who was killed. Claudius, who had sailed with the armies as far as France, had returned to Rome, but after receiving a prearranged signal involving a series of beacons, he sailed to Britain with extra reserves and the war elephants that had already been shipped to Boulogne. The elephants carried arms and supplies and lifted away the brushwood that been placed in the soldiers' path. The British had never seen elephants before and in the final push into Colchester the soldiers scattered.

Claudius himself rode into Colchester on the back of an elephant. He swore honourable alliance with the Kings of the Icenians, East Kent, and East Sussex, who had assisted him in the campaign. The remainder of Caractacus' kingdom he formally declared a Roman province (p. 265). He left Britain after 16 days, leaving Aulus in charge as governor. On his return, the Senate agreed that a triumphal procession should take place and this was arranged for the following year. A second, but lesser, triumph took place four years later when Aulus returned from Britain bringing the captured King Caractacus with him. Caractacus made such a noble speech to Claudius that instead of executing him he freed him to live as his guest in Rome (pp. 342-3).

KING HEROD AGRIPPA

Claudius received a series of letters from Vibius Marsus, the Roman governor of Syria, raising concerns about the activities of King Herod Agrippa. He reported first that he was fortifying Jerusalem, then that he had invited a number of neighbouring kings to a secret meeting (pp. 231-3). None of these kings had called on Vibius Marsus to offer their respects to Claudius, as they should have done.

Claudius believed the reports but kept things on a friendly basis with Herod Agrippa, writing to ask him questions about the prophesied messiah, who was expected by the Jewish people. It subsequently emerged that Herod Agrippa had come to believe that he himself was the messiah and that his role was to free the Jews from the yoke of Rome.

Herod Agrippa died shortly after addressing the crowd gathered in the amphitheatre at Caesarea for the celebration of Claudius' birthday. Before he died, he wrote a letter to Claudius admitting that had plotted to take the Eastern Empire away from Rome, but that he loved his old friend "more truly than you ever supposed" (p. 304).

DEATH OF MESSALINA

Seven years after he became emperor, Claudius discovered that his wife Messalina had been conducting affairs and political intrigues behind his back. After coming to him with a strange story about a prophesy that her husband would be killed, she went through a form of marriage with Silius, the consul-elect, whom Claudius disliked. Claudius had initially agreed to the idea on the basis that the couple would not actually consummate the marriage. He realised he had been deceived when reports reached him of the drunken behaviour of Messalina and her guests at the wedding party. Details of her other affairs emerged and the shocked Claudius was given a sedative by his doctor, Xenophon. The order for Messalina's execution was given by Narcissus (p. 385).

MARRIAGE TO AGRIPPINILLA

Three months later Claudius married another manipulative woman, his niece Agrippinilla. The marriage was political and Agrippillina took over much of the official work of the empire. She poisoned him in CE 54 after five years of marriage.

CHARACTER STUDY

THE EMPEROR CLAUDIUS

Claudius had suffered from poor health as a child, and as an adult he stammered and limped. His family had treated him as a fool and it was this that had kept him safe from his "ambitious and bloody-minded relatives", who did not consider him "worth the trouble of executing, poisoning, forcing to suicide, banishing to a desert island or starving to death" (p. 9). When Caligula was assassinated, Claudius was discovered by the palace guards hiding behind a curtain.

Prior to his accession as emperor he had led a quiet life, studying and writing history. Like his father and grandfather, he held republican views and initially refused to become emperor. However, once he was established, he rose to the challenge and did some good things for Rome, such as the building of much-needed aqueducts and the enlarging of the Port of Ostia. His success in the conquest of Britain was the highlight of his reign and gained him much-needed respect.

He was susceptible to influence by those he felt close to. Prior to her downfall, he trusted his wife Messalina, who was politically astute, to sign and seal documents on his behalf without reading them first. It came as a great shock to him when he discovered Messalina's deceit and scheming. He gave his freedmen ministerial positions and, as with Messalina, was shocked when one of them (Polybius) let him down. He ordered the execution of Polybius, whom he had made Minister of Arts, because Messalina found proof that he had been selling citizenships. The freedmen who served Claudius formed a "very close guild" (p. 336) and the others were affronted by his death. Later Claudius discovered that Messalina had been having an affair with Polybius and that he was jealous of her new love, the actor Mnester (pp. 335-6).

KING HEROD AGRIPPA

Herod Agrippa was educated in Rome as a friend of the Imperial family. He studied with Claudius under his tutor Athenodorus and the two remained friends. Claudius' mother, Antonia, had a lot of affection for the young man Claudius called a "scoundrel with a golden heart" (p. 15) and helped him when he got into serious debt. He was imprisoned by Claudius' uncle, the Emperor Tiberius, for making remarks Tiberius considered to be treasonable. When Tiberius died his successor, Caligula, released him from prison and gave him the Tetrarchy of Bashan and its revenues and the title of king (p. 49). He was in Rome at the time of Caligula's assassination and his quick thinking helped avert a massacre by the German Household Battalion, who were supporters of Caligula.

When Herod Agrippa returned home the two friends wrote to one another, using their schoolboy nicknames. Herod Agrippa's was Brigand, and Claudius' was Marmoset. Herod Agrippa had warned Claudius to trust nobody, but Claudius did not think that included Herod Agrippa himself. When reports came that he was fortifying Jerusalem and building alliances with neighbouring kings, Claudius was not sure what to make of it. It transpired that his old friend had begun to think of himself as the expected Jewish messiah and believed that it was his duty to free the Jewish people from Roman domination.

King Herod Agrippa is a major character in *Claudius the God*. Apart from a brief recap of Claudius' accession as emperor, the first four chapters of the book are given over to a history of Herod Agrippa's family and the background to the friendship between the two men.

MESSALINA

Messalina was Claudius' third wife and he was passionately in love with her. Their son Drusus (later called Britannicus) was born three weeks after Claudius became emperor and a daughter, Octavia, followed less than a year later. Claudius was disappointed when Messalina asked if they could sleep separately from now on as she did not want to have any more children yet. She moved out of Claudius' new palace into the old one, where she set up separate quarters. She assured Claudius that she still loved him and they continued to work together. Claudius even allowed her to give orders on his behalf and issued her with a seal so she could sign documents as though they were from him. It was seven years before he discovered that she was deceiving him with a string of other lovers. Her deceptions eventually led to her execution.

AGRIPPILLINA

Agrippillina was Claudius' fourth and last wife, whom he married three months after the death of Messalina. Agrippillina was Claudius' niece (daughter of his brother Germanicus) and he had to gain permission from the Senate to marry her. As a young woman, Agrippillina and her sister Lesbia had been banished by their brother, Caligula, with whom she was said to have committed incest. At the suggestion of Messalina, she had been allowed to return to Rome after Claudius became emperor. Agrippillina's first husband was Domitius Ahenobarbus, who had the reputation of being "the bloodiest-minded man in Rome" (p. 349). He was a cruel man who, when congratulated on the birth of his son (the future Emperor Nero), said: "If you had any patriotism you would go to the cradle and strangle the child at once. Don't you realise that Agrippinnilla and I between us command all the known vices, human and inhuman?" *(ibid.).* The marriage between Agrippinnilla and Claudius was not a love match; in fact, he seems to have actively disliked her and married her solely because of her political acumen.

ANALYSIS

GENRE: HISTORICAL NOVEL

Claudius the God, like its prequel, *I, Claudius*, is a historical novel: in other words, a work of fiction based on a real historical situation. A historical novel may have a mix of fictional and real characters, and the events can be a mixture of what is known or believed to be true and what comes solely from the writer's imagination. Robert Graves initially conceived the Claudius novels as an "interpretive biography" (Seymour, 1995: 214), but instead wrote a fictional autobiography, a first person account that gives Claudius his own voice.

The novels were extremely well-researched. Graves drew on more than 25 Roman writers, including Suetonius and Tacitus, as well the Emperor Claudius himself in his surviving letters and speeches (p. 7). He writes: "Few incidents here are wholly unsupported by historical authority of one sort or another and I hope none are historically incredible. No character is invented" (*ibid.*). Striving for authenticity, Graves inserted translations of two of Claudius' surviving writings in the novel: *Claudius' Edict about certain Tyrolean Tribes A.D. 46*, and *Surviving Fragments of Claudius' Speech to the Senate, Proposing the Extension of the Roman Citizenship to the French of Autun District* (pp. 359-362). He also added, at the end, translations of three versions of Claudius' death: those of Suetonious, Tacitus and Dio Cassus (pp. 427-439).

Graves' method when working on a historical novel was to immerse himself in the era he was writing about. He had the ability to imagine his way into the past, a process he called the "analeptic method" (Seymour, 1995: 315). His biographer, Miranda Seymour, suggests that while he was writing the Claudius novels he: "became Claudius, so his subject inevitably came to share some of his author's habits and obsessions" (*ibid.*: 216).

RELIGION

It is certainly not difficult to draw parallels between the fictional Claudius and his creator Robert Graves. Claudius is very interested in religion, for example. We might expect that of an emperor who is also the chief pontiff of Rome and priest of the defied Emperor Augustus, but the novel goes further. There is a lengthy explanation of the rituals of the druids (pp. 219-225), the sources for which were: "archaeological works, ancient Celtic literature, and modern megalithic culture in the New Hebrides where the dolmen and Menhir are still ceremonially used" (p. 8), there being very little on the subject in the classical sources. In the novel, Claudius cites the Druidic cult as one of the reasons he went to war with Britain, as he believed the influence of the Druids on the people of Northern France was checking "the progress of civilization" (p. 219) there, at a time when he wanted to extend Roman citizenship in Gaul. Graves' own interest in ancient religion and mythology can be seen in *The White Goddess: A Historical Grammar of Poetic Myth* (1948).

Claudius' conversations with Herod Agrippa on Judaism and its emergent off-shoot, Christianity, find their parallel later on in Graves' discussions with Joshua Podro, a Polish Jewish intellectual whom he met when he was working on *King Jesus* (1946).

In the novel Claudius notes a "notable breakdown in religious belief after our conquest of Greece, when Greek philosophy spread to Rome" (p. 292). As Claudius saw it, the philosophers had converted gods such as Jove, Mercury, Venus and Diana into remote philosophical concepts of "Power, Intelligence, Beauty and Chastity" *(ibid.)*, leaving the ordinary citizen, who needed intermediary beings, with a void. Into this void, Claudius said, came foreign gods with definite personalities who "satisfied people's emotional needs" (p. 295). Examples are the Egyptian goddess Isis and god Serapis *(ibid.)*, who had a double temple in Rome.

Claudius himself loved "ancient forms and ceremonies and [had] an inherited belief in the old Roman Gods" (p. 294), which he refused "to subject to philosophical analysis" *(ibid.)*. As priest of Augustus, he distinguished between Augustus the man and Augustus the deity. However, he felt that the worship of Augustus as a major deity at Rome would not have been possible without the gulf opened up by the philosophers (p. 295).

Claudius began an investigation into the foreign gods. He forbade Roman citizens to attend the

Jewish synagogues and expelled the most enthusiastic Jewish missioners (p. 296). He wrote to Herod Agrippa to tell him what he had done and Herod Agrippa replied that he thought he had acted wisely, and that he in turn intended to prevent Greek teachers of philosophy holding classes in Jewish cities *(ibid.)*. Followers of Joshua ben Joseph (Jesus) had made considerable headway in the empire, even in Rome itself. Aulus Plautius' wife had been accused of attending one of their "love feasts" while her husband was away in Britain, but Claudius "hushed up the affair for his sake" (p. 309). He later arrested all the leading Christians in Rome and the Orthodox Jewish missionaries and sent them out of the country (p. 339).

CHANGING BEHAVIOUR

Having reluctantly accepted his position as emperor, Claudius resolved to rule honourably and reversed some of Caligula's harsh edicts. However, as time went on he began to behave more like his predecessors, Caligula and Tiberius. Responding to Messalina's suspicions of a conspiracy against him, he tried the Senator Asiaticus in his own study instead of bringing him before the Senate, leaving Asiaticus with no choice but to commit suicide (p. 332). He ordered the execution of the young Pompey, husband of his daughter Antonia (by his second wife, Aeilia Paetina) without a trial, as he was cheating on her with a male lover and had failed to consummate their marriage (pp. 334-5).

Claudius broke down after the death of Messalina. Devastated when the full extent of her disloyalty to him was revealed, he gave over the decision on how to handle the situation to his freedmen. It was Narcissus who ordered her death. He married Agrippillina, the choice of his freedman Pallas, three months after Messalina's death.

In the end Claudius seems to have given up:

> "I have let Agrippillina and my freedmen rule me. I have opened and shut my mouth and gestured with my arms like the little marionettes they make in Sicily: but the voice has not been mine, nor the gestures. I must say Agrippillina has shown herself a remarkable ruler of the tyrannical sort [...] The fact is that I got tired of being Emperor. I wanted someone to do the

> work for me. I married [Agrippillina] not for [her] heart but for [her] head. It takes a woman to run an empire like this" (pp. 399-400).

This was an extraordinary comment for a Roman Emperor to make. Claudius is remembering his grandmother Livia, who was married to the Emperor Augustus. Livia had been a woman of whom it was said: "Augustus rules the Empire but Livia rules Augustus" (Graves, 1978: 24). Claudius had hated her but in the end he came to respect her. Livia had been determined that her son, Tiberius, would become emperor after Augustus died and she achieved this by a combination of manipulation and the murder of his rivals. In the same way, Agrippinilla was determined that her son, Nero, would succeed Claudius instead of his own son, Brittanicus.

At first her plans seemed to be going well. Claudius adopted Nero and decided to send Britannicus to Britain, safe from the scheming of Rome. However, Britannicus did not want this. He asked Claudius to make him a joint heir with Nero and give him tutors who would train him in public speaking, finance and legal procedure, skills he would need if he became emperor.

Claudius agreed to do this and recommended both Nero and Britannicus to the Senate. Agrippinilla acted quickly. Claudius died shortly afterwards, poisoned by Agrippinilla, just as Livia before her had poisoned her husband, Augustus.

FURTHER REFLECTION

SOME QUESTIONS TO THINK ABOUT...

- Robert Graves initially thought of writing the Claudius novels as an "interpretative biography". What do you think of his decision to write them as autobiography instead? Does the first person account make the story more 'real' to you, or would you have preferred a more detached, third person narrative?
- After the Emperor Caligula was assassinated, Claudius declared that he did not want to become emperor; he would prefer Rome to revert instead to a Republic, as it had been in the past. Do you think his protest was genuine?
- When Claudius accepted his position as emperor, he believed that he would be much better placed than the consuls (who only served for one year) to rebuild Rome after the destructive reign of Caligula (p. 82). To what extent do you think he succeeded in doing so?

- How important do you feel the role of King Herod Agrippa is to the story?
- Claudius' freedmen formed a "very close guild" (p. 336). To what extent do you think the execution of one of their group (Polybius) might have influenced their attitude towards Messalina?
- What do you think of Narcissus' decision to order Messalina's execution?
- Do you think Claudius was unwise in handing so much power to his freedmen? Explain your answer.
- What do you think the attitude of the Senate and the people was to Claudius after his conquest of Britain?
- As the years went on, Claudius became more tyrannical. What do think was the reason for this?

We want to hear from you!
Leave a comment on your online library
and share your favourite books on social media!

FURTHER READING

REFERENCE EDITION

- Graves, R. (1978) *Claudius the God*. London: Penguin.

REFERENCE STUDIES

- Graves, R. (1978) *I, Claudius*. London: Penguin.
- Seymour, M. (1995) *Robert Graves: Life on the Edge*. London: Doubleday.

ADDITIONAL SOURCES

- Alston, R. (1998) *Aspects in Roman History, AD 14 -117*. London: Routledge.
- Beard, M. & Crawford, M. (1999) *ROME IN THE LATE REPUBLIC: Problems and Interpretations*. London: Duckworth.
- Fagan, G. G. (No date). Claudius (41-54 A.D.). *De Imperatoribus Romanis*. [Online]. [Accessed 26 January 2019]. Available from: <http://www.roman-emperors.org/claudius.htm>

- Lending, J. (2018). Herod Agrippa 1 (44 CE). *Livius. Culture, history and literature.* [Online]. [Accessed 26 January 2019]. Available from: <https://www.livius.org/articles/religion/messiah/messianic-claimant-8-king-herod-agrippa-i/>

- Levick, B. (1990) *Claudius.* Yale: Yale University Press.

- Suetonius, G. (revised) (2007) *The Twelve Caesars.* Translated by Robert Graves and revised by James B. Rives. London: Penguin Books.

ADAPTATIONS

- *I, Claudius.* (1976) [Television Miniseries]. UK: British Broadcasting Corporation.

MORE FROM BRIGHTSUMMARIES.COM

- Reading guide – *Goodbye to All That* by Robert Graves.

- Reading guide – *I, Claudius* by Robert Graves.

www.brightsummaries.com

Ebook EAN: 9782808017602

Paperback EAN: 9782808017619

Legal Deposit: D/2019/12603/47

Cover: © Primento

Digital conception by Primento, the digital partner of
publishers.